TAKING THE HIGH ROAD
to Reading, Writing, and Listening

Book 3-1

By Arlene Capriola and Rigmor Swensen

Phoenix Learning Resources

St. Louis • New York

ACKNOWLEDGEMENTS

Teachers at the Fifth Avenue Elementary School in East Northport, New York, expressed a need for supplementary materials to practice skills required for the new, more demanding curriculum. We responded to the request and spent many more hours than we had ever anticipated to create *Taking the High Road*.

The staff and students followed through, piloting and critiquing our manuscripts. To their credit, they made no concessions to our egos. They were very clear about what worked and what didn't.

Thank you, teachers and students at Fifth Avenue Elementary, and special thanks to Josephine Imwalle, Donna Marenus, and Francesca Montague. With gratitude and affection, we dedicate these books to all of you.

"Rain in the Night," from *Time for Poetry*, Scott Foresman, 1951

Cover and interior page design: Pencil Point Studio
Illustrations: Ray Skibinski

Copyright © 1999 By Phoenix Learning Resources, Inc. All Rights Reserved. Printed in the United States of America. No part of this publication may be reproduced, stored in a retrieval system, or transmitted, in any form or by any means, electronic, mechanical, photocopying, recording, or otherwise, without prior written permission of the publisher.

ISBN: 0-7915-1646-6

7 8 9 10 11 09 08 07 06

TABLE OF CONTENTS

A Science Article: **The Emperor Penguin** 1
    Objective Questions: Critical Thinking
    Using the Information: Short Answer Format
    Pre-Writing: Using a **5 W's Chart**
    Writing: Newspaper Article

A Biography: **Young Jimmy Carter** 9
    Objective Questions: Critical Thinking
    Using the Information: Short Answer Format
    Pre-Writing: Using a **Flow Chart**
    Writing: Designing a Flow Chart

A Poem: **Rain in the Night** 19
    Objective Questions: Critical Thinking
    Using the Information: Short Answer Format
    Pre-Writing: Using a **Schedule**
    Writing: Personal Narrative

A Social Studies Article: **Two Countries—Two Markets** 27
    Objective Questions: Critical Thinking
    Using the Information: Short Answer Format
    Pre-Writing: Using a **Venn diagram**
    Writing: Compare and Contrast

Listening Comprehension: **An Ancient Greek Folktale, "King Midas"** 37
    Listening Directions: **Story Map**
    Using the Information: Short Answer Format
    Writing: Drawing a Conclusion

A Study Skill: **Reading a Recipe** 41
    Objective Questions: Critical Thinking
    Pre-Writing: **Make your own Recipe**
    Illustration

A Correspondence: **Letter to the Town Board** 45
    Objective Questions: Critical Thinking
    Using the Information: Short Answer Format
    Pre-Writing: Using a **Mind Map**
    Writing: Business Letter

A Fable: **The Boy Who Cried Wolf** 53
    Objective Questions: Critical Thinking
    Using the Information: Short Answer Format
    Pre-Writing: **Story Map**
    Writing: Summary

A Study Skill: **Street Maps** 63
    Objective Questions: Critical Thinking

Editor's Page 65
Guide for **Revising** and **Editing** essays

A Science Article

THE EMPEROR PENGUIN

What I Know

Fill in the correct circle.

1. Penguins are _____.
   ○ fish   ○ birds

2. The story says that the father emperor penguin "plays a role" in hatching the egg. This means that he _____.
   ○ plays a song   ○ has a part

3. This story is nonfiction. This means that it is _____.
   ○ make-believe   ○ true facts

Check the Answer Box to see!

What I Want to Know

(✔ Check all that you want to know.)

❑ How big this penguin is
❑ Where the penguins live
❑ What the penguins eat
❑ _____

(go on)

ANSWER BOX
1. Penguins are birds.
2. "Plays a role" means has a part.
3. Nonfiction means that it has true facts.

THE EMPEROR PENGUIN

Emperor penguins are strange birds. The boy and girl penguins look alike. They have thick black and white feathers. This makes them look like little men all dressed up for a fancy party. Penguins need heavy feathers to keep warm. Their home is on the ice shelf in **Antarctica**[1], where there is only ice and snow.

Penguins are birds that cannot fly. When they are on land, they waddle or hop along. Sometimes they slide across the ice on their bellies. But they love to be in the water. Then they dip and swirl through the waves. They can zoom up to 30 miles an hour.

THE ROOKERY

The emperor penguin is the largest of all penguins. It gets to be almost 4 feet tall and can weigh as much as 75 pounds. Up to half a million emperor penguins live together in a big group called a rookery. They feed on the fish, squid, and shrimp they catch in the ocean. But they have to be careful. Killer whales and leopard seals swim in the cold waters around the Antarctic. They like to eat penguins. Penguins have to be on their guard on land, too. Huge birds called skuas prey on them. They steal penguin eggs and **swoop**[2] up the little chicks.

[1]**Antarctica**: continent at the South Pole   [2]**swoop**: fly down and grab

FATHER PENGUIN STANDS GUARD

Emperor penguins are different from other penguins in one special way. The father has the biggest role in hatching the eggs. In the winter the mother lays just one egg. Then she dives into the sea to find food. The father penguin stays with the egg. He holds it on his feet. His warm belly covers the egg, making it very warm and comfortable. He stands like that for 62 to 64 days. There are many winter storms. At times the temperature goes way below zero degrees. But he stays in the same spot and does not eat the whole time. By the time the egg is ready to hatch he is very skinny.

THE BABY IS BORN

In the spring, the mother emperor penguin returns to the rookery. The baby penguin hatches. The little chick is all gray and **downy**[3]. Now the father can leave to find food. The mother takes over. She puts her beak over the baby's beak. Then food comes up from her stomach to feed the penguin chick. She feeds the baby in this way until it is strong enough to fish for its own food.

[3]**downy**: soft and fluffy

What I Learned

Circle the letter next to the answer you choose for each question.

1. Killer whales are the penguin's _____ .
    a. friend
    b. enemy
    c. parent
    d. teacher

2. Why does the father penguin become skinny?
    a. The fish are hard to catch.
    b. He goes on a diet.
    c. He cannot leave the egg.
    d. The mother gives him food.

3. The father penguin holds the egg about _____.
    a. 2 weeks
    b. 2 months
    c. 2 days
    d. 2 years

4. In the story we can tell that a "rookery" is _____ . (Hint: the word "called" is a signal word. It tells us that a definition is coming.)
    a. food for the penguin
    b. the penguin baby
    c. half a million
    d. a big group

5. How is the penguin different from most other birds?
    a. It cannot fly.
    b. It is short.
    c. It loves the water.
    d. It is black and white.

6. What is this story is mostly about?
    a. all kinds of birds
    b. one special kind of bird
    c. what a mother penguin eats
    d. the cold waters of the Antarctic

7. In the first paragraph, the author compares the penguin to _____ .
    a. a man dressed for a party
    b. a man with heavy feathers
    c. the ice shelf in the Antarctic
    d. a killer whale

8. We can tell from this article that the emperor penguin moves _____ .
    a. better on land
    b. around in the sun
    c. better in the water
    d. as slow as the turtle

Using the Information Use the information from the story to answer each question.

- -

1. Explain how the father penguin helps take care of the baby.

_____

_____

_____

_____

2. Tell at least two ways that the penguin is different from most other birds.

_____

_____

_____

_____

Using the Information

3. Why do penguins have to be careful on land and sea?

_____

_____

_____

_____

_____

4. In the box below, show two ways the Emperor Penguin travels on land.

Pre-Writing You are a news reporter for "The New York Lines" newspaper. A baby emperor penguin has just been born. Use the facts in this story to tell about it in the 5 W's Chart below.

WHO is the article about?	Baby emperor penguin
WHAT has just happened?	
WHEN did it take place?	
WHERE did it happen?	
HOW did it look when it came out?	

Writing Read the facts in your 5 W's Chart. Write a newspaper article telling about the birth of the penguin.

The New York Lines

Late Animal Edition

"All the news we wish to tell"   Fifty cents

BABY EMPEROR PENGUIN BORN

Go to Editor's Page

A Biography

YOUNG JIMMY CARTER

What I Know

Fill in the correct circle.

1. A biography is _____ .
   ○ the story of someone's life   ○ a kind of science

2. Jimmy Carter was _____ .
   ○ a famous inventor   ○ the President of the U.S.

3. Jimmy Carter grew up _____ .
   ○ in New York City   ○ on a peanut farm

Check the Answer Box to see!

What I Want to Know

(✔ Check all that you want to know.)

❑ What Jimmy Carter did as a boy
❑ Where he grew up
❑ Who else was in his family
❑ _____

(go on)

ANSWER BOX
1. A biography is the story of someone's life.
2. Jimmy Carter was the President of the U.S.
3. Jimmy Carter grew up on a peanut farm.

YOUNG JIMMY CARTER

Jimmy Carter was the 39th president of the United States. He is a very famous man. But not many people know about what he was like when he was a little boy.

When Jimmy was a boy, he lived on a peanut farm in Georgia. He spent a lot of time around the farm, playing with his brother and two sisters. One day he asked his dad if he could have some of the peanuts. He wanted to go into business. His dad said, "Go ahead and good luck."

Jimmy took a red wagon down to the peanut field. There the peanuts grow on the roots of vines. One vine can have up to fifty nuts on it. So Jimmy worked all morning. He dug up vines until his wagon was filled to the brim.

When he got home, he dumped the nuts into a big barrel of water. The next morning, Jimmy boiled them in salt water. While they cooled off, he went to get 20 bags. It didn't take long to fill each bag.

Then Jimmy was off to market. He took the shortcut along the railroad tracks. But it was still two miles into the town of Plains. Lots of people loved those boiled peanuts. They looked for him every Saturday. And he always sold all of his bags.

Young Jimmy Carter was a very successful businessman. And he was only six years old!

What I Learned

Circle the letter next to the answer you choose for each question.

1. This story tells about Jimmy Carter when he was a _____
    a. young man
    b. President of the U.S.
    c. little boy
    d. playmate

2. When he was six years old, Jimmy Carter was very _____
    a. clever
    b. dumb
    c. tall
    d. artistic

3. Where do peanuts grow?
    a. on trees
    b. on the roots
    c. on the leaves of vines
    d. in little bushes

4. Why did Jimmy dump the nuts into a barrel of water?
    a. to wash them
    b. to hide them
    c. to boil them
    d. to cool them

5. How did Jimmy get the peanuts to market?
    a. His dad drove him.
    b. He took the railroad.
    c. The people took him.
    d. He walked alone.

6. Jimmy Carter was good at his business because he _____
    a. was lucky
    b. got help from his dad
    c. worked hard
    d. had a brother

7. What did Jimmy's dad think about Jimmy's business?
    a. He thought Jimmy should play instead.
    b. He was jealous.
    c. He was too busy to care.
    d. He encouraged him.

8. Which of these is an opinion?
    a. Carter was the 39th President.
    b. Jimmy sold peanuts.
    c. Businessmen make good presidents.
    d. Carter grew up in Georgia.

Using the Information Use the information from the story to answer each question.

1. Tell how young Jimmy got started in the peanut business.

_____

_____

_____

_____

2. How did Jimmy's father help him succeed?

_____

_____

_____

_____

Using the Information

3. Give at least two reasons why Jimmy became a successful businessman.

_____

_____

_____

_____

_____

4. In the box below, draw a picture of a peanut plant growing in the ground.

Making a Flow Chart

Jimmy Carter followed a lot of steps to get his peanuts to market. In the boxes below follow each step of the job.

The pictures will help you!

First Jimmy _____

_____

Then he _____

_____

The **next** morning _____

_____

Making a Flow Chart

After they cooled, Jimmy _____

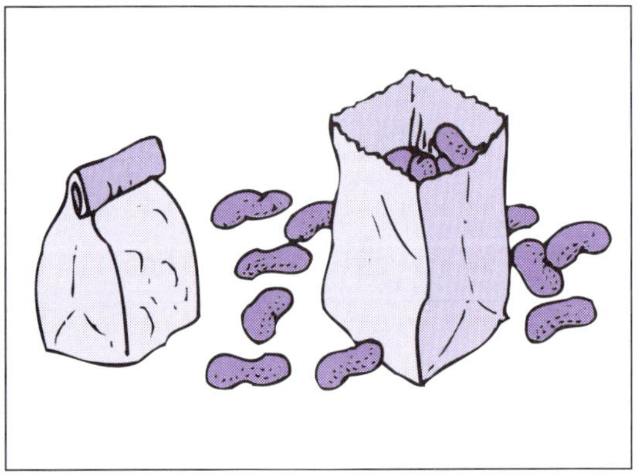

Then he _____

Finally _____

16

Writing Jimmy Carter had to follow many steps to take the peanuts from the ground and sell them in town. The FLOW CHART at the end of the story helped us to show this. The words **first, then, next, after,** and **finally** helped us tell the story in order.

■■■■■■■■■■■■■■■■■■■■■■■■■■■■■■■■■■■■■■

Think of something you do that takes a few steps. Then tell about it in the flow chart below. Use the key words above. Make a picture to go with each step. You can choose from these ideas or make up your own:
- ○ Making a sandwich   (example: peanut butter and jelly)
- ○ Playing a game   (example: checkers)
- ○ Planting a flower   (example: from a packet of seeds)
- ○ _____

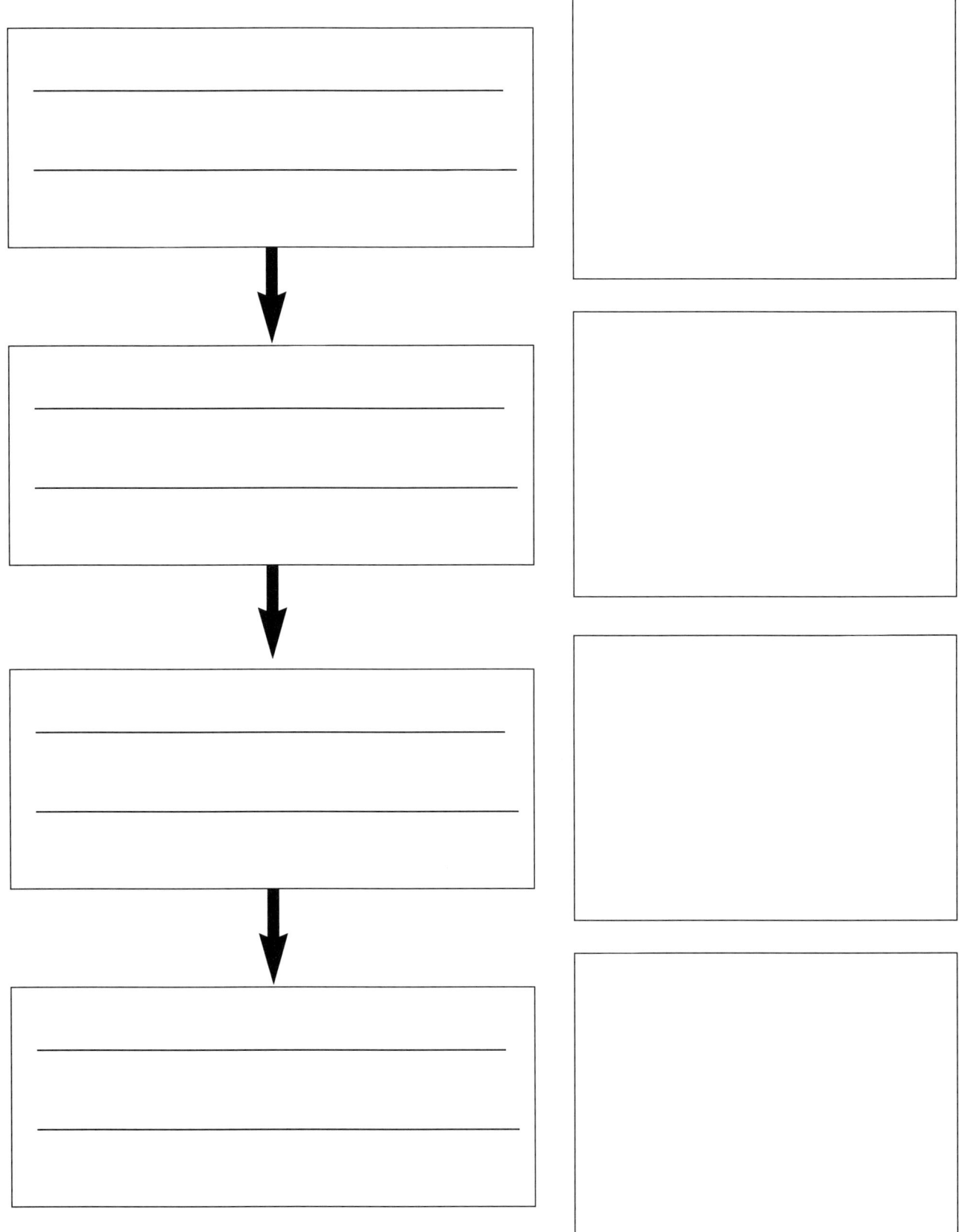

A Poem
RAIN IN THE NIGHT

What I Know

Fill in the correct circle.

1. A poet is someone who _____ .
   ○ writes a poem   ○ works for the post office

2. Pansies are a kind of _____ .
   ○ cookie   ○ flower

3. When two words rhyme, they have the same _____ .
   ○ ending sound   ○ beginning sound

Check the Answer Box to see!

What I Want to Know

(✔ Check all that you want to know.)

❑ How many stanzas are in this poem
❑ If the lines rhyme
❑ What happens to pansies in the rain
❑ _____

(go on)

ANSWER BOX
1. A poet is someone who writes a poem.
2. Pansies are a kind of flower.
3. Rhyming words have the same ending sound.

RAIN IN THE NIGHT

Rain can be fun; rain can be beautiful.
Do you feel the same as this poet about the rain?

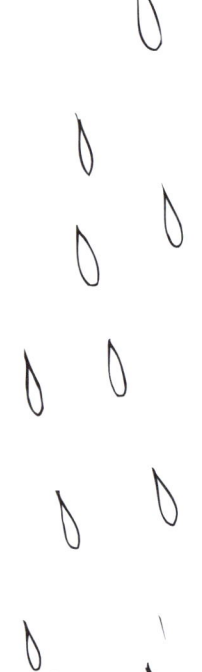

Raining, raining,
All night long;
Sometimes loud, sometimes soft,
Just like a song.

There'll be rivers in the gutters
And lakes along the street.
It will make our lazy kitty
Wash his little dirty feet.

The roses will wear diamonds
Like kings and queens at court;
But the pansies all get muddy
Because they are so short.

I'll sail my boat tomorrow
In wonderful new places,
But first I'll take my watering-pot
And wash the pansies' faces.

by Amelia Josephine Burr

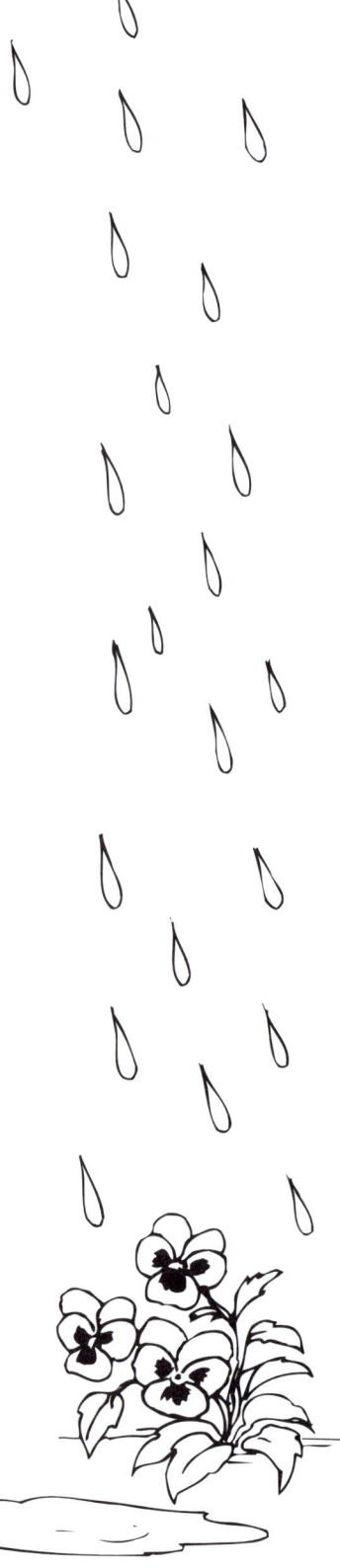

What I Learned

Circle the letter next to the answer you choose for each question.

1. When does this poem take place?
   - a. morning
   - b. tomorrow
   - c. night
   - d. afternoon

2. Why do the pansies get muddy?
   - a. They bend down.
   - b. They are very tall.
   - c. They are short.
   - d. The kitty has dirty feet.

3. How will the rain help the kitten?
   - a. It will make him stay in.
   - b. It will wash his dirty dish.
   - c. It will keep the dog away.
   - d. It will clean his paws.

4. How does this poet feel about the rain?
   - a. She does not like it.
   - b. She's afraid of it.
   - c. She likes it.
   - d. She thinks it makes many problems.

5. What is the first thing the poet will do the next day?
   - a. sail a boat
   - b. wash the pansies
   - c. clean the kitten
   - d. see the diamonds

6. "The roses will wear diamonds" means that the roses _____.
   - a. have diamonds on the petals
   - b. belong to kings and queens
   - c. have raindrops that shine like diamonds
   - d. have a diamond shape

7. Why will there be "wonderful new places" to sail her boat?
   - a. There will be deep puddles.
   - b. She'll go to the river.
   - c. There will be water in the bathtub.
   - d. The rain will sing a song.

8. Where is the poet?
   - a. in school
   - b. playing in the sunshine
   - c. inside a house
   - d. at the river

Using the Information Use the information from the story to answer each question.

1. The poet says that rain is like a song. What do you think she means?

_____

_____

_____

_____

2. Why does the poet want to wash the pansies? Explain.

_____

_____

_____

_____

Using the Information

3. Tell about any two "new wonderful places" the poet could sail the boat.

_____

_____

_____

_____

_____

4. In the box below, draw a picture of how the street looked after the rain.

Pre-Writing The poet was planning what she would do the next day. Pretend it has rained all night where you live. The sun will come out the next day and it will be a perfect Saturday. Plan what you will do to have a wonderful day of fun.

■ ■

Write your plan in the schedule below. Do not fill in each line. Some things will take more than one hour.

SATURDAY SCHEDULE

9:00 - _____

10:00 - _____

11:00 - _____

12:00 - _____

1:00 - _____

2:00 - _____

3:00 - _____

4:00 - _____

5:00 - _____

6:00 - _____

Writing Pick one thing you planned to do. Write a paragraph for each one. Tell all about it. Use exciting words to show how great it will be.

_____ – _____
　　　(time)　　　　　　　　　　　(activity)

Go to Editor's Page

_____
(activity)

Draw a picture of you doing one of the activities you wrote about.

A Social Studies Article

TWO COUNTRIES, TWO MARKETS

What I Know

Fill in the correct circle.

1. Farsi is the name of the _____ .
   - ○ language of Iran
   - ○ park in Chicago

2. A vendor is someone who _____ .
   - ○ buys something
   - ○ sells something

3. A stall is like a little _____ where things are sold.
   - ○ shed
   - ○ tree

Check the Answer Box to see!

What I Want to Know

(✔ Check all that you want to know.)

- ❑ Where Iran is
- ❑ What the market in Iran is like
- ❑ What the second country is
- ❑ _____→

(go on)

ANSWER BOX
1. Farsi is the language of Iran.
2. A vendor is someone who sells something.
3. A stall is like a little shed where things are sold.

27

TWO COUNTRIES, TWO MARKETS

People all over the world shop for the things they need. Some of their customs are alike, and some are very different. Read about a very large shopping market in Iran, a country in Asia.

The Central Bazaar

Thousands of people come from far away to the Central Bazaar, a marketplace in Iran. It covers more than five miles of streets. Here shoppers can see the goods in little booths or stalls. They try to get the best **bargain**[1], calling out in their Farsi language.

Vendors set up their stalls by sections. In one section there is nothing but rugs. Another will have only **pottery**[2]. All the clothes, leather, jewels, and food booths will be in their own areas.   Even water sellers have booths. The one thing that is missing, though, is a section for restaurants. There are none. Food is bought at the market and taken home to eat.

Shopping at the bazaar takes a long time. The stalls that the shopper wants to visit may be in opposite directions. A long walk may separate them. Shoppers are tired after a day at the market.

[1]**bargain**: price agreed to   [2]**pottery**: pots, dishes, or jars made from baked clay

28

Here is an article about a large shopping center in the United States. How is it like the one in Iran? How is it different?

The Mall of America

The Mall of America is one of the largest shopping malls in the United States. It covers one square mile. Thousands of people come from far away to shop there. Most speak English. The indoor mall has stores on three levels. Elevators and **escalators**[3] carry shoppers from place to place.

Big department stores are found in all sections of the mall. They sell clothes, toys, jewelry, and **housewares**[4] within one store. All items for sale are marked with tags that tell the price. There is no bargaining for a better price.

Fancy restaurants serve breakfast, lunch, and dinner. For the shopper in a hurry, there is a food court with hamburgers and hot dogs, ice cream, and many other foods. In the center of these stands are tables and chairs. Customers, tired from a day of shopping, can sit and rest. Right in the middle of the mall is an amusement park, with rides for kids of all ages.

[3]**escalators**: stairways with moving steps   [4]**housewares**: things for the home

What I Learned

Circle the letter next to the answer you choose for each question.

1. What is this story mainly about?
   a. markets in two different countries
   b. how to bargain
   c. learning languages
   d. different kinds of food

2. What language is spoken at the Central Bazaar?
   a. French
   b. Farsi
   c. English
   d. Spanish

3. Where would you buy a rug at the bazaar?
   a. at a stall
   b. in the department store
   c. from a pottery vendor
   d. on the second level

4. What do you do when you "bargain" for a rug at the bazaar?
   a. pay the price on the ticket
   b. meet the rug weaver
   c. talk and agree on the price
   d. pick the colors

5. How are the bazaar and the mall alike?
   a. They are in the same country.
   b. Thousands of people come to both.
   c. They both have restaurants.
   d. They both have places to play.

6. How is the mall different from the bazaar?
   a. The mall has three levels.
   b. The mall is very large.
   c. The mall sells many things.
   d. The mall shoppers get tired.

7. If you were going to bargain for an item, you would have to_____.
   a. know the vendor
   b. know how much it is really worth
   c. pay the price on the tag
   d. speak English

8. Why do you think there is an amusement park in the mall?
   a. The salespeople get bored.
   b. It makes a lot of noise.
   c. It makes kids like to come shopping.
   d. People eat hot dogs there.

Using the Information Use the information from the story to answer each question.

1. Tell about one problem you might have shopping at the bazaar.

2. What is the difference in how things are priced at the bazaar and at the mall?

Using the Information

3. Would you rather shop at the Bazaar or at the Mall of America? Explain why.

_____

_____

_____

_____

_____

4. Draw one vendor's stall at the Bazaar. Show what he sells.

Pre-Writing A **Venn diagram** helps us to see clearly how things are alike and different. But first we have to decide just what is alike and what isn't.

■ ■

To help you decide, we have listed some things you can compare in the two markets. On the line, put A if they are alike in the two countries and D if they are different.

I started you off!

__A__	how many people come
__D__	what each shop sells
_____	how shoppers get from place to place
_____	how shoppers feel after a day of shopping
_____	where people eat
_____	what language is spoken
_____	the size of the markets
_____	what the shops look like
_____	what children can play on
_____	where the shoppers come from
_____	how they decide the price
_____	_____
_____	_____

You are ready to put your information into the Venn Diagram, below. Now you know which things are alike and which are different. Explain each one in just a few words.

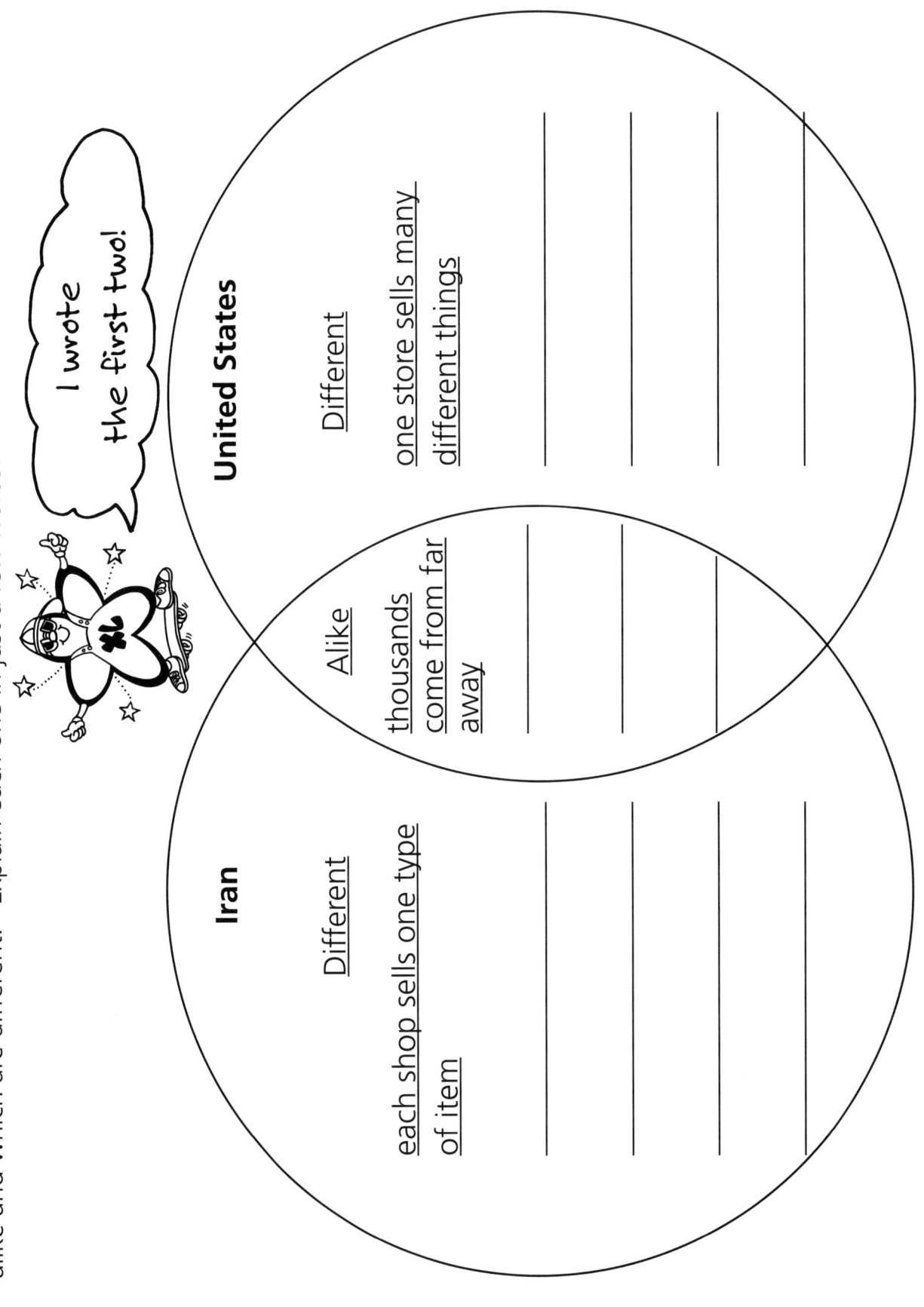

I wrote the first two!

Iran

Different

each shop sells one type of item

Alike

thousands come from far away

United States

Different

one store sells many different things

Writing Now it is easy to compare the two markets. Finish the report below. Use your Venn Diagram to help you.

You may add other things, too!

   The Central Bazaar in Iran and the Mall of America in the United States are alike in some ways. Both _____

_____

_____

_____

_____

The two markets are different in many ways, too. _____

_____

_____

_____

_____

35

Draw a picture showing something you wrote about.

Go to Editor's Page

Listening Comprehension
KING MIDAS

Listening Directions

Listen to the Greek folktale "King Midas." The first time you hear it, listen carefully but do not write anything. The second time you hear the story, fill in the **story map**, below. It will help you answer some questions about the story.

Main Characters: _____

_____

_____

What is Midas's problem? _____

_____

What happens? _____

_____

_____

_____

How it ends: _____

_____

Using the Information Use the information from the story to answer each question.

■■■■■■■■■■■■■■■■■■■■■■■■■■■■■■

1. How do you know that King Midas was a good man?

_____

_____

_____

_____

2. What happens in the story that cannot happen in real life?

_____

_____

_____

_____

Using the Information

3. What did King Midas mean when he said, "I am cured of my greed"?

_____

_____

_____

_____

_____

4. Draw a picture of King Midas's daughter right after she touched him.

Writing Which lesson below does this story teach?
- ○ Greed can make a good thing turn bad.
- ○ Be careful of what you touch.

Write an essay explaining why you chose this lesson.

Use details from your story map in this essay!

Go to Editor's Page

A Study Skill

READING A RECIPE

Here is a recipe for a dessert called Apricot Rounds, a favorite in Iran.

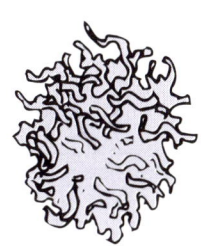
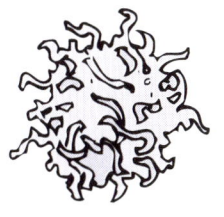

Apricot Rounds

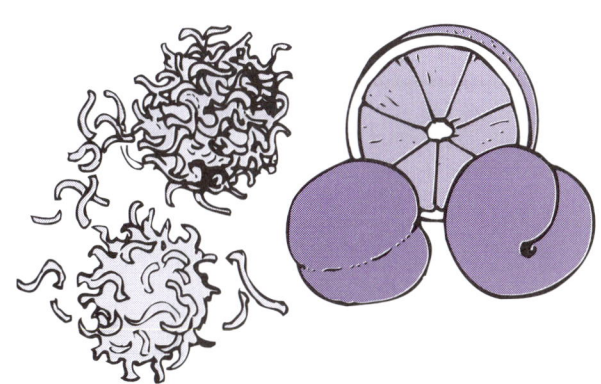

Ingredients:
1 orange
1 (lb) pound of dried apricots
1/3 (c) cup of sugar
4 (oz) ounces of shredded coconut

How to Prepare:

1. Peel orange and take out the seeds.
2. Grind apricots and the orange together.
3. Stir in sugar.
4. Leave uncovered for 1/2 hour or until sugar is melted.
5. Shape mixture into balls the size of a Ping-Pong ball.
6. Roll in coconut and place in cookie dish.
7. Serve at room temperature.

Makes about a dozen tasty treats

What I Learned

Fill in the answer for each question.

1. A _____ tells you how to prepare something to eat.

2. How many ingredients do you need to make this recipe? _____

3. To prepare the Apricot Rounds, first you must _____
   _____

4. After you grind the fruit, you _____

5. The abbreviation for ounces is _____

6. The letters lb. stand for _____

7. Apricot Rounds should be as big as _____

8. How long do you leave the mixture uncovered? _____
   _____

9. Do you have to cook to make this recipe? _____

10. Should the Apricot Rounds be hot when you serve them? _____

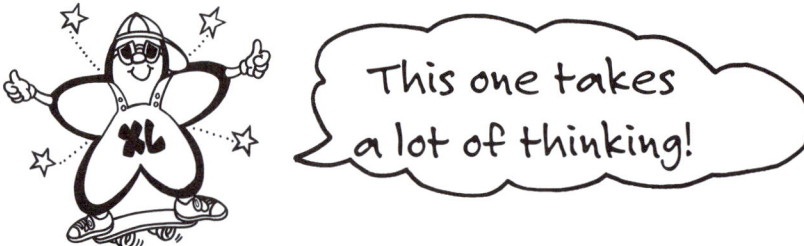

This one takes a lot of thinking!

The Apricot Rounds must be _____ to keep the coconut on.

Make Your Own Recipe

Most people love to share and trade recipes for the special things they like to make. What do you know how to make—without looking at a recipe first. Write the recipe for it below.

You can pick one of my favorites or think of your own!

- ◯ a sandwich (I know lots)
- ◯ an ice cream sundae
- ◯ lemonade
- ◯ Jell-o
- ◯ pizza
- ◯ _____

Ingredients:

_____

_____

_____

How to Prepare:

_____

_____

_____

An Illustration Many cookbooks have illustrations (pictures) to show what the food will look like when it is done. Make an illustration of the food for which you wrote the recipe. Place it on a fancy dish.

_____
(name of food)

A Correspondence

LETTER TO THE TOWN BOARD

What I Know

Fill in the correct circle.

1. A business letter has a special _____ .
   - ○ form
   - ○ stamp

2. A business letter usually is _____ .
   - ○ funny
   - ○ serious

3. We mostly write business letters to _____ .
   - ○ our friends
   - ○ people we may not know

Check the Answer Box to see!

What I Want to Know

(✔ Check all that you want to know.)

- ❑ Who wrote this letter
- ❑ What he or she wants to tell the town board
- ❑ How a business letter looks
- ❑ _____

(go on)

ANSWER BOX
1. A business letter has a special form.
2. A business letter usually is serious.
3. We mostly write business letters to people we may not know.

45

LETTER TO THE TOWN BOARD

Peter McDunn
15 Fleet Drive
Cove Center, Maine 97841
June 15, 1998

Mr. Harold Strong, Chairman
Town Board
112 Main Street
Cove Center, Maine 97841

Dear Mr. Strong:

My friends Linda, Juan, and I play at the Sunset Park Playground. We meet lots of kids there. We like to play ball and go on the jungle gym. But it is very hot in the summer and there is no swimming pool. There is no place to take swimming lessons.

If we had a swimming pool, more of the kids would spend their afternoons at the park. This is a safe, fun place for kids to be. Our parents would not have to worry about the traffic on the streets. Many kids would watch less T.V. in the afternoons and get exercise instead. If we had swimming lessons, we could all learn to be good swimmers, too.

We have collected 100 names of kids who would like to have a swimming pool at the playground. Please vote on this at your next meeting.

Send your answer to me. I will tell everyone else. We hope to hear from you very soon.

Yours truly,

Peter Mc Dunn

Peter McDunn

Mr. Harold Strong, Chairman
Town Board
112 Main Street
Cove Center, Maine 97841

August 12, 1998

Peter McDunn
15 Fleet Drive
Cove Center, Maine 97841

Dear Peter:

The Town Board talked about your request for a pool at the Sunset Park playground.   The community will vote on it at the next election.

We will need to tell the community how to get the money for the pool. Do you have any ideas? Can you and your friends help in any way? Please let us know.

Yours truly,

Harold Strong
Harold Strong, Chairman

Using the Information Use the information from the story to answer each question.

1. Was it a good idea for Peter to write to the town board? Explain.

2. The kids collected 100 names. Why was this a good idea?

Using the Information

3. Do you think the kids will get the swimming pool? Tell why or why not.

_____

_____

_____

_____

4. In the box below, draw the park as it was described in the letter. Show where you think the pool should be built.

Pre-Writing Mr. Strong needs ideas to get the money to build the town's swimming pool. What can kids do to raise money? Think of ways. Maybe you have already done something to get money for your school, church or temple, or club. The mind map below will help you think of things. Put in all your ideas.

- Chores
- Make and Sell
- Raffle
- You fill in

Ways to raise money

Writing Write a letter back to Mr. Strong. Tell him some of your ideas for getting the money for the swimming pool. Look back to find the correct business form.

Go to Editor's Page

A Fable

THE BOY WHO CRIED WOLF

What I Know

Fill in the correct circle.

1. A fable is a story that _____ .
   ○ teaches a lesson   ○ always has a happy ending

2. When sheep "graze," they _____ .
   ○ feed on grass   ○ are really talking

3. The story says the wolf "licks his lips." This means that he ____.
   ○ is angry   ○ is thinking of a good meal

Check the Answer Box to see!

What I Want to Know

(✔ Check all that you want to know.)

❑ Why the boy cries wolf
❑ What the wolf in the story does
❑ What lesson this story teaches
❑ _____

(go on) →

ANSWER BOX
1. A fable is a story that teaches a lesson.
2. When sheep "graze," they feed on grass.
3. When someone "licks his lips," he is thinking of a good meal.

THE BOY WHO CRIED WOLF

Once upon a time, there was a boy who lived in a small village. His father had many sheep. Most of the villagers kept sheep. But there was no place in town for the sheep to graze.

Outside the village was a big hill. The sheep liked to eat the tall, green grass that grew on the side of the hill. It made them big, fat, and woolly. But who would watch the sheep way out there and keep them safe from the hungry wolf?

The people of the village asked the young boy to tend them. "You will be near the town," they said. "You have a very important job. Keep the sheep out of trouble. Do not let them get stuck in the bushes. Be sure not one of them gets lost."

"Most of all protect them from the big, bad wolf. He licks his lips when he thinks he can grab a lamb for supper. If he does, soon we will have no meat to eat. There will be no wool to make sweaters and coats to wear in the winter."

The boy promised to be on guard. And he was, for a while. Then he realized there were no boys and girls to play with. There were no games to play. And there was no wolf in sight. He was bored.

"I'll play a trick on all the people in town. I will cry, Wolf! Wolf! The wolf is here!" he thought. "Then at least someone will come up here."

That is what he did. The people grabbed sticks, stones, bricks, and bats and ran helter-skelter up the hill. They did not find a wolf. The boy said it was just a joke.

The villagers didn't think it was funny. They were angry. They grumbled as they went back to work.

The boy felt badly. He did his job very carefully for a whole week. Then he was bored and lonely again. "Wolf, Wolf!", he shouted. "The wolf is eating the sheep!"

This time the villagers ran really fast, carrying their sticks, stones, bricks, and bats. They were sure the wolf had come.

Once again, the boy said, "It was just for fun. I wanted people to come up and see me."

This time the villagers didn't even stop to scold him. They had to hurry back to work. They were very angry. But they could not find another boy to take care of the sheep.

The boy's father made him promise he would never do it again. He felt ashamed. For a whole week he kept his eye on those sheep.

Suddenly, from the corner of his eye, he saw a big, hungry wolf. He got so scared, he screamed. "Help! Help! Run! Run! The wolf is eating the sheep!"

But the people in the village did not listen. They went on working. They said to each other, "That boy is a pest. He must think we are very silly to come running for the third time."

So the wolf had a feast. He gobbled up as many sheep as he could.

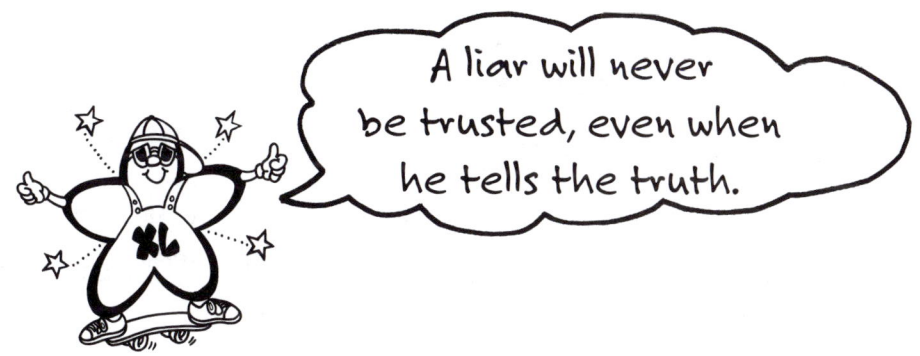

A liar will never be trusted, even when he tells the truth.

What I Learned

Circle the letter next to the answer you choose for each question.

1. This story tells about what happened when a boy_____.
   a. played
   b. was honest
   c. lied
   d. liked wolves

2. Why did the boy play a trick on the people of the town?
   a. He got lonely.
   b. He was hungry.
   c. He was afraid.
   d. He got sick.

3. When did a real wolf come?
   a. the first time the boy called
   b. the second time he called
   c. the third time he called
   d. the fourth time he called

4. The story says the people ran "helter-skelter" up the hill. This means they were _____.
   a. funny
   b. in a rush
   c. old
   d. late

5. Why didn't the people come the last time he called?
   a. They were not home.
   b. They were tired.
   c. They did not have time.
   d. They did not believe him.

6. What will happen because the wolf came?
   a. The people will have no meat.
   b. There will be a party.
   c. There will be lots of wool.
   d. The wolf will be hungry.

7. What lesson does this story tell?
   a. It is fun to play tricks.
   b. Wolves are sneaky.
   c. People don't believe those who lie.
   d. Sheep are dull animals.

8. How does the boy probably feel at the end of the story?
   a. happy
   b. ashamed
   c. friendly
   d. clever

Using the Information Use the information from the story to answer each question.

1. Why did the villagers need the sheep?

_____

_____

_____

_____

2. The villagers told the boy to watch out for three kinds of trouble. What were they?

_____

_____

_____

_____

Using the Information

3. What do you think will happen when the villagers see that the sheep have been eaten?

_____

_____

_____

_____

_____

4. Show what the boy did when the villagers ran up the hill the first time.

60

Pre-Writing Sometimes it is hard to retell a story. Maps help us to put things in order. A Story Map helps us to get all the important parts of the story straight. Fill in the story map for the story you just read.

If you forgot one part, take a peek back!

Title: _____

Setting: _____

Characters: _____

Boy's problem: _____
_____

First time he: _____ How it turns out: _____

Second time he: _____ How it turns out: _____

Third time: _____ How it turns out: _____
_____

What lesson does he learn? _____
_____

61

Writing Now it is easy to retell the story "The Boy Who Cried Wolf." Use your story map to tell all the important parts of the story. This is called a summary.

Can you make it fit on this one page?

Go to Editor's Page

A Study Skill

READING A STREET MAP

A Street Map helps us to find our way in a neighborhood. The map below shows some of the streets in the town of Fort Hill. The Map Key tells us what each symbol means. Study this map. How many places can you find?

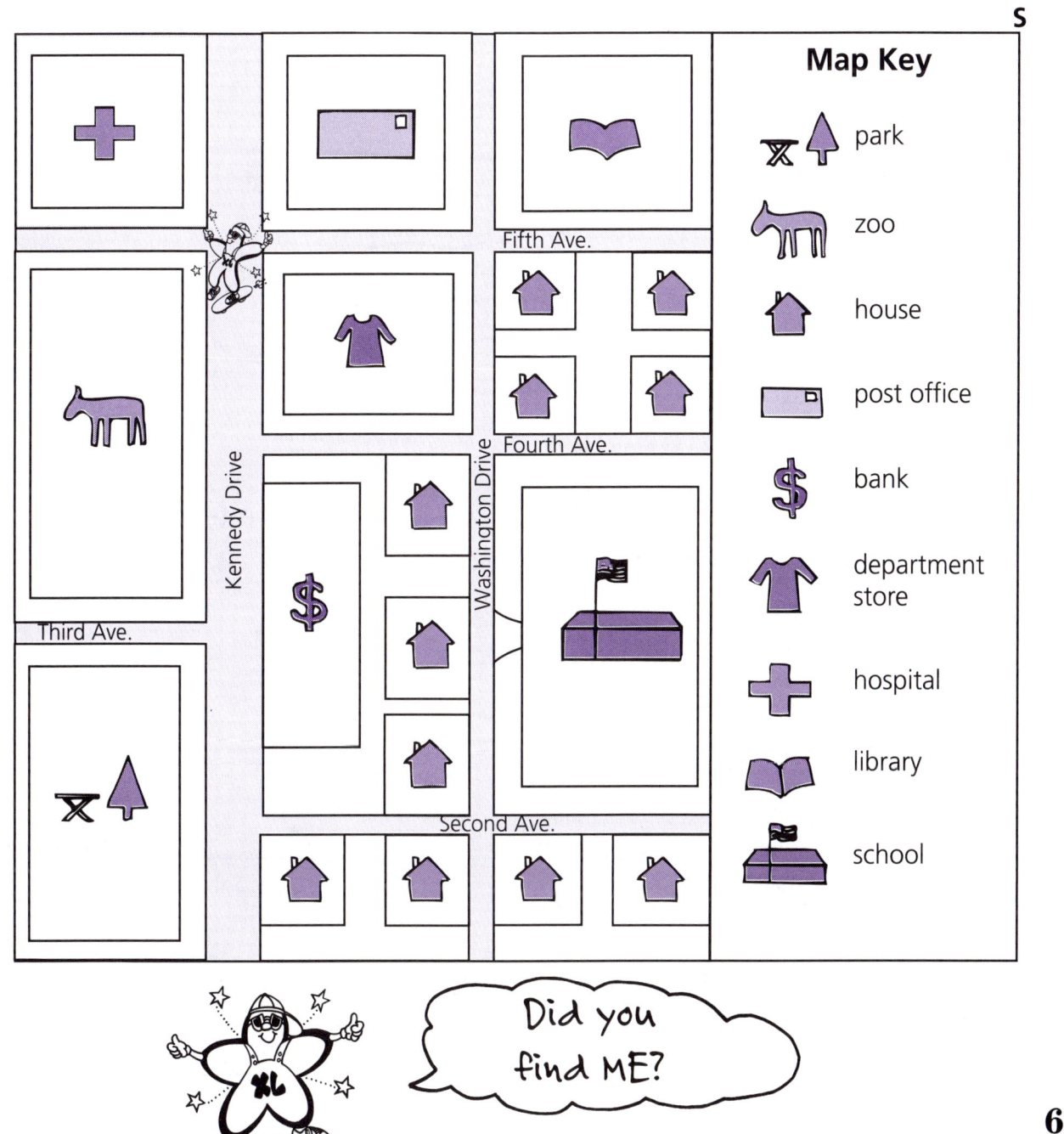

What I Learned

Write north, south, east, or west for sentences 1 to 5.

1. The school is on the _____ side of town.

2. If I go from school to the library, I walk _____ .

3. The zoo is _____ of the department store.

4. When I go from the park to the zoo, I am traveling _____ .

5. The post office is on the _____ side of town.

6. All the streets that go north to south are named after _____ .

7. All the avenues are named after _____ .

8. How many houses are there? _____

9. When I leave the zoo, I cross _____ to get to the bank.

10. I walk from the hospital to the library. What building do I pass on my left? _____

64

EDITOR'S PAGE

WOW! You wrote a good story! Now its time to upgrade it from good to great! XL will show you how.

Go to a quiet spot. Read your story aloud.

Y   N   **Did you stick to the topic?**
(Just cross out the sentences that don't belong!)

Y   N   **Does each sentence make sense?**
Did you leave out any words you meant to write? (Put this ^ and add them now.)

Y   N   **Did you use interesting words**
(Try to think of 5 more exciting ones and change them!)

Y   N   **Did you use the same tired word over and over again?**
(A thesaurus has lots of synonyms for a quick change!)

Now share your story with a friend. Bet it sounds much better!

Check your writing for errors. Ask a friend to help.

Y N **Is there correct punctuation after each sentence?**
(Remember: each sentence needs a . or ? or !)

Y N **Does every sentence and name start with a capital?**

Y N **Did you spell the words correctly?**
(This is the part a friend can really help with!)

Now you have finished! Do you want to share your story with others? If you do, it needs to be "cleaned" up a bit. Copy it with all the changes onto a clean sheet of paper.